THE EOS LIFE

Journal and Planner

Name: ______________________________

Email: ______________________________

Phone: ______________________________

Year: ______________ Quarter: ______________

GET STARTED

The EOS Life Journal and Planner is designed to be a companion to *The EOS Life* book by Gino Wickman. The book will create the context for the journal sections of this journal and planner.

1. Read *The EOS Life* by Gino Wickman
2. Complete Chapters 1 through 5 while reading the book
3. Begin using the planner daily to stay on track living your EOS Life
4. Carry your journal and planner with you everywhere you go
5. Subscribe to receive a new planner every quarter at www.eoslife.com/subscribe

BENBELLA

BenBella Books, Inc.
10440 N. Central Expressway
Suite 800
Dallas, TX 75231
benbellabooks.com
Send feedback to feedback@benbellabooks.com

ISBN 978-1-63774-601-1

Printed in China
10 9 8 7 6 5 4 3 2 1

CONTENTS

How long are you going to wait before you demand the best for yourself?

—Epictetus

Date:

Doing What
I Love
With People
I Love
Making A
Huge
Difference
Being
Compensated
Appropriately
With Time
For Other
Passions

Chapter 1

DOING WHAT YOU LOVE

"Where your talents and the needs of the world cross, lies your calling, vocation, purpose."
—Aristotle

WHAT DO YOU LOVE TO DO?

Please take a few minutes right now and ponder this question. Write down everything that comes to mind.

Doing what you love rating (1–10): ____

LAUNDRY LIST

Date: ____________

List out everything you've done over the past few weeks. Transfer to Delegate and Elevate™.

DELEGATE AND ELEVATE™

Date:

Love / Great	Like / Good

Don't Like / Good	Don't Like / Not Good

What are your top delegations this quarter? At least one per quarter:

What	Who	By When

THE ACCOUNTABILITY CHART™

Date:

What is the one thing you can delegate within the next 7 days?

Chapter 2

WITH PEOPLE YOU LOVE

"You will either look back in life and say I wish I had, or I'm glad I did."
—Zig Zigler

WHO ARE THE PEOPLE YOU LOVE WORKING WITH?

Please take a few minutes right now and ponder this question. Write down everything that comes to mind.

With people you love love rating (1–10): _____

THE PEOPLE ANALYZER™

Date: ______________

Name							

List out the next actions you will take to surround yourself with people you love.

Chapter 3

MAKING A HUGE DIFFERENCE

"The people who are crazy enough to think they can change the world are the ones who do."

—Steve Jobs

HOW DO YOU MAKE A DIFFERENCE?

Please take a few minutes right now and ponder this question. Write down everything that comes to mind.

Making a huge difference rating (1–10): ____

VISION / TRACTION ORGANIZER™

Date:

Core Values

-
-
-
-
-

Core Focus™

Purpose / Cause / Passion:

Niche:

10-Year Target™

Marketing Strategy

Target Market / "The List":

3 Uniques™:

1.
2.
3.

Proven Process:

Guarantee:

VISION / TRACTION ORGANIZER

Date:

3-Year Picture™

Future Date:

Revenue:

Profit:

Measureables:

VISION / TRACTION ORGANIZER

Date:

1-Year Plan

Future Date:

Revenue:

Profit:

Measureables:

Goals for the Year

Rocks

Future Date:

Revenue:

Profit:

Measureables:

What	Who

Issues List

MAKING A DIFFERENCE

Date:

Write how you want to make a difference in the world. What action will you take in the next 7 days?

Chapter 4

BEING COMPENSATED APPROPRIATELY

"Those who do more than they are paid for, will sooner or later be willingly paid for more than they do."
—Napoleon Hill

HOW ARE YOU ADDING/CREATING VALUE?

Please take a few minutes right now and ponder this question. Write down everything that comes to mind.

Being compensated appropriately rating (1–10): ____

BEING COMPENSATED APPROPRIATELY

Date:

Current Compensation	Desired Compensation

What will you do to add more value to the world to achieve your desired compensation?

Chapter 5

WITH TIME TO PURSUE OTHER PASSIONS

"The difference between successful people and *really* successful people is that really successful people say no to almost everything."
—Warren Buffett

WHAT ARE YOUR PASSIONS OUTSIDE OF WORK?

Please take a few minutes right now and ponder this question. Write down everything that comes to mind.

Time to pursue other passions rating (1–10): ____

THE PERSONAL V/TO™

NAME: ______________________

VISION

<table>
<tr><td rowspan="5">CORE VALUES</td><td colspan="2">1.
2.
3.
4.
5.</td><td rowspan="5">3-YEAR PICTURE™

Future Date:
Income:
Net Worth:
Measurables:
What does it look like?
•
•
•
•
•
•
•
•
•
•
•
•
•
•
•
•
•
•
•</td></tr>
</table>

<table>
<tr><td>CORE VALUES</td><td colspan="2">1.
2.
3.
4.
5.</td></tr>
<tr><td>PERSONAL CORE FOCUS™</td><td colspan="2">Purpose:

Niche:</td></tr>
<tr><td>10-YEAR TARGET™</td><td colspan="2"></td></tr>
<tr><td>LIFETIME WISH LIST</td><td>•
•
•
•
•
•
•
•
•</td><td>•
•
•
•
•
•
•
•
•</td></tr>
<tr><td>CORE HABITS</td><td>•
•
•
•
•</td><td>•
•
•
•
•</td></tr>
</table>

THE PERSONAL V/TO™

NAME: ____________________

TRACTION

1-YEAR PLAN	ROCKS (the next 90 days)	ISSUES LIST
Future Date: **Income:** **Net Worth:** **Measurables:** **Goals for the Year:** 1. ____ 2. ____ 3. ____ 4. ____ 5. ____ 6. ____ 7. ____ With your cursor in the last row, press Tab to add another row.	**Future Date:** **Income:** **Net Worth:** **Measurables:** **Rocks for the Quarter:** 1. ____ 2. ____ 3. ____ 4. ____ 5. ____ 6. ____ 7. ____ With your cursor in the last row, press Tab to add another row.	**Ideas, problems, concerns, obstacles, and barriers** 1. ____ 2. ____ 3. ____ 4. ____ 5. ____ 6. ____ 7. ____ 8. ____ 9. ____ 10. ____ 11. ____ 12. ____ 13. ____ With your cursor in the last row, press Tab to add another row. **Prioritize** **- Identify** **- Discuss** **- Solve**

TIME TO PURSUE PASSIONS

Date:

Weekly Working Container	Working Weeks per Year

Personal Passions

What will you do in the next 7 days to begin creating time to pursue passions?

Chapter 6

THE JOURNEY

"Life is about the journey, not the destination."
—Ralph Waldo Emerson

WHAT DOES YOUR IDEAL LIFE LOOK LIKE?

Please take a few minutes right now and ponder this question. Write down everything that comes to mind.

PLANNER INSTRUCTIONS

Quarterly

- ☐ Update your Vision/Traction Organizer after your quarterly session.
- ☐ Complete your Delegate and Elevate.
- ☐ Think about your EOS Life.

Weekly

- ☐ Take a Clarity Break™ every week. Just take time away from the office to simply think. Document your thoughts in your planner.
- ☐ Review your prior week. What did you learn? What will you do differently? Reflection is the key to learning.
- ☐ Create your weekly plan by reviewing your V/TO, Personal V/TO™, the prior week's notes, and to-dos, and clearing all inboxes.
- ☐ Document your 3 biggest wins for the week. What would make it a successful week for you?

Daily

- ☐ Before going to bed each night, create your plan for the next day. Your brain will do amazing things while you sleep and the next day will be more productive.
- ☐ Document the 3 biggest to-dos and your daily schedule. Make sure to build in flexibility and don't over-schedule yourself.
- ☐ Upon waking, execute the plan as you defined it. Know that it will never go perfectly.
- ☐ Capture notes and new to-dos on the Daily Notes page.
- ☐ At the end of each day, reflect on what you would do differently. Learn from what worked and what didn't. Review your new to-dos and notes and create your plan for the next day.
- ☐ Rinse and repeat daily.

CLARITY BREAK

One discipline that all great leaders practice is taking time on a regular basis to rise above the everyday demands of their jobs to reflect and think at the thirty-thousand-foot level.

To stay sharp, confident, and at your best for your people, you must take Clarity Breaks. By definition, a Clarity Break is time you schedule away from the office, out of the daily grind of running the department, to think and to work on your business, department, or self.

Stepping back to think will create clarity for you and restore your confidence. This is important because the normal course of day-to-day business pulls you deeper and deeper into the minutiae of your work. As a result, you sometimes can't see the forest for the trees. You start to feel overwhelmed and you become short with your people.

Make the time to save time.

Therefore, at intervals, you must elevate yourself above the day-to-day activities "in" the business so you can work "on" the business. Schedule an appointment with yourself. Put it down on your calendar. If you don't schedule the time, it will never magically happen. At first you may be concerned about when you'll find the time. The irony is, you'll actually save time by taking Clarity Breaks. When you are clear about your bigger objectives, you gain the confidence to simplify procedures and create efficiencies.

Minimize distractions and allow yourself to just think.

Use this scheduled break wisely, though. This is not time to catch up on email or complete a to-do list. It's time to think, to see things clearly, and to restore your confidence. Faced with a blank legal pad or journal, with no agenda, interruptions, or distractions, you'll be challenged at first to actually think. Use these Clarity Break questions to get started.

Clarity Break Questions

- *Is the Vision and Plan for the business/department on track?*
- *What is the number one goal?*
- *Am I focusing on the most important things?*
- *Do I have the Right People in the Right Seats to grow?*
- *What is the one "people move" that I must make this quarter?*
- *How strong is my bench?*
- *If I lose a key player, do I have someone ready to fill the seat?*
- *Are my processes working well?*
- *What seems overly complicated that must be simplified?*
- *Do I understand what my direct reports truly love to do and are great at doing?*
- *Am I leveraging their strengths?*
- *What can I delegate to others in order to use my time more effectively?*
- *What can we do to be more proactive versus being reactive?*
- *What can I do to improve communication?*
- *What's my top priority this week? This month?*

CLARITY BREAK

CLARITY BREAK

WEEKLY REVIEW

Week of: ____________ to ____________

☐ *Review Level 10 Meeting™ notes* ☐ *Review Quarterly Rocks*

☐ *Review last week's calendar*

What worked last week:

What didn't work last week:

Knowing what you know now, what will you do differently next week?

What were your 3 biggest wins last week, and why?

Looking over the past week, what are you most grateful for?

WEEKLY PLAN

Week of: ______ to ______

☐ *Review V/TO* ☐ *Review Personal V/TO* ☐ *Review last week's notes and to-dos*

☐ *Clear all inboxes*

What are your 3 biggest wins for next week?

○

○

○

How many hours will you work next week?

How do you plan to eat next week?

How do you plan to exercise next week?

How do you plan to connect with friends and family next week?

What are your key appointments and ideal outcomes for next week?

Date and Time	Appointment	Desired outcome

DAILY PLAN

Date: ____________

☐ *Practice Stillness*

What are your 3 key to-dos?

○
○
○

Other to-dos

Daily Schedule

Notes, issues, and reflections

DAILY NOTES

Date: ____________

DAILY PLAN

Date: ______

☐ *Practice Stillness*

What are your 3 key to-dos?

○ ______
○ ______
○ ______

Other to-dos

Daily Schedule

Notes, issues, and reflections

DAILY NOTES

Date:

DAILY PLAN

Date:

☐ *Practice Stillness*

What are your 3 key to-dos?

○

○

○

Daily Schedule

Other to-dos

Notes, issues, and reflections

DAILY NOTES

Date:

DAILY PLAN

Date: ____________

☐ *Practice Stillness*

What are your 3 key to-dos?

○ ____________
○ ____________
○ ____________

Other to-dos

Daily Schedule

Notes, issues, and reflections

DAILY NOTES

Date:

DAILY PLAN

Date:

☐ *Practice Stillness*

What are your 3 key to-dos?

○
○
○

Other to-dos

Daily Schedule

Notes, issues, and reflections

DAILY NOTES

Date:

DAILY PLAN

Date:

☐ *Practice Stillness*

What are your 3 key to-dos?

○

○

○

Other to-dos

Daily Schedule

Notes, issues, and reflections

DAILY NOTES

Date:

DAILY PLAN

Date:

☐ *Practice Stillness*

What are your 3 key to-dos?

○

○

○

Daily Schedule

Other to-dos

Notes, issues, and reflections

DAILY NOTES

Date:

The price of greatness
is responsibility.

—Winston Churchill

CLARITY BREAK

Clarity Break Questions

- *Is the Vision and Plan for the business/department on track?*
- *What is the number one goal?*
- *Am I focusing on the most important things?*
- *Do I have the Right People in the Right Seats to grow?*
- *What is the one "people move" that I must make this quarter?*
- *How strong is my bench?*
- *If I lose a key player, do I have someone ready to fill the seat?*
- *Are my processes working well?*
- *What seems overly complicated that must be simplified?*
- *Do I understand what my direct reports truly love to do and are great at doing?*
- *Am I leveraging their strengths?*
- *What can I delegate to others in order to use my time more effectively?*
- *What can we do to be more proactive versus being reactive?*
- *What can I do to improve communication?*
- *What's my top priority this week? This month?*

CLARITY BREAK

CLARITY BREAK

WEEKLY REVIEW

Week of: ______ to ______

☐ *Review Level 10 Meeting notes*
☐ *Review Quarterly Rocks*
☐ *Review last week's calendar*

What worked last week:

What didn't work last week:

Knowing what you know now, what will you do differently next week?

What were your 3 biggest wins last week, and why?

Looking over the past week, what are you most grateful for?

WEEKLY PLAN

Week of: ______ to ______

☐ *Review V/TO* ☐ *Review Personal V/TO* ☐ *Review last week's notes and to-dos*

☐ *Clear all inboxes*

What are your 3 biggest wins for next week?

○ ______

○ ______

○ ______

How many hours will you work next week?

How do you plan to eat next week?

How do you plan to exercise next week?

How do you plan to connect with friends and family next week?

What are your key appointments and ideal outcomes for next week?

Date and Time	Appointment	Desired outcome

DAILY PLAN

Date: __________

☐ *Practice Stillness*

What are your 3 key to-dos?

◯ __________

◯ __________

◯ __________

Other to-dos

Daily Schedule

Notes, issues, and reflections

DAILY NOTES

Date:

DAILY PLAN

Date:

☐ *Practice Stillness*

What are your 3 key to-dos?

○

○

○

Other to-dos

Daily Schedule

Notes, issues, and reflections

DAILY NOTES

Date:

DAILY PLAN

Date: ____________

☐ *Practice Stillness*

What are your 3 key to-dos?

○ ____________

○ ____________

○ ____________

Other to-dos

Daily Schedule

Notes, issues, and reflections

DAILY NOTES

Date:

DAILY PLAN

Date: ______

☐ *Practice Stillness*

What are your 3 key to-dos?

○ ______

○ ______

○ ______

Other to-dos

Daily Schedule

Notes, issues, and reflections

DAILY NOTES

Date:

DAILY PLAN

Date:

☐ *Practice Stillness*

What are your 3 key to-dos?

○

○

○

Daily Schedule

Other to-dos

Notes, issues, and reflections

DAILY NOTES

Date:

DAILY PLAN

Date:

☐ *Practice Stillness*

What are your 3 key to-dos?

○

○

○

Daily Schedule

Other to-dos

Notes, issues, and reflections

DAILY NOTES

Date: ____________

DAILY PLAN

Date: ____________

☐ *Practice Stillness*

What are your 3 key to-dos?

○ ____________
○ ____________
○ ____________

Other to-dos

Daily Schedule

Notes, issues, and reflections

DAILY NOTES

Date: __________

The best revenge is massive success.

—Frank Sinatra

CLARITY BREAK

Clarity Break Questions

- *Is the Vision and Plan for the business/department on track?*
- *What is the number one goal?*
- *Am I focusing on the most important things?*
- *Do I have the Right People in the Right Seats to grow?*
- *What is the one "people move" that I must make this quarter?*
- *How strong is my bench?*
- *If I lose a key player, do I have someone ready to fill the seat?*
- *Are my processes working well?*
- *What seems overly complicated that must be simplified?*
- *Do I understand what my direct reports truly love to do and are great at doing?*
- *Am I leveraging their strengths?*
- *What can I delegate to others in order to use my time more effectively?*
- *What can we do to be more proactive versus being reactive?*
- *What can I do to improve communication?*
- *What's my top priority this week? This month?*

CLARITY BREAK

CLARITY BREAK

WEEKLY REVIEW

Week of: ____________ to ____________

☐ *Review Level 10 Meeting notes* ☐ *Review Quarterly Rocks*

☐ *Review last week's calendar*

What worked last week:

What didn't work last week:

Knowing what you know now, what will you do differently next week?

What were your 3 biggest wins last week, and why?

Looking over the past week, what are you most grateful for?

WEEKLY PLAN

Week of: __________ to __________

☐ *Review V/TO* ☐ *Review Personal V/TO* ☐ *Review last week's notes and to-dos*

☐ *Clear all inboxes*

What are your 3 biggest wins for next week?

○

○

○

How many hours will you work next week?

How do you plan to eat next week?

How do you plan to exercise next week?

How do you plan to connect with friends and family next week?

What are your key appointments and ideal outcomes for next week?

Date and Time	Appointment	Desired outcome

DAILY PLAN

Date: ______

☐ *Practice Stillness*

What are your 3 key to-dos?

◯ ______

◯ ______

◯ ______

Other to-dos

Daily Schedule

Notes, issues, and reflections

DAILY NOTES

Date:

DAILY PLAN

Date:

☐ *Practice Stillness*

What are your 3 key to-dos?

○

○

○

Other to-dos

Daily Schedule

Notes, issues, and reflections

DAILY NOTES

Date:

DAILY PLAN

Date:

☐ *Practice Stillness*

What are your 3 key to-dos?

○

○

○

Other to-dos

Daily Schedule

Notes, issues, and reflections

DAILY NOTES

Date:

DAILY PLAN

Date:

☐ *Practice Stillness*

What are your 3 key to-dos?

○

○

○

Other to-dos

Daily Schedule

Notes, issues, and reflections

DAILY NOTES

Date:

DAILY PLAN

Date: ______

☐ *Practice Stillness*

What are your 3 key to-dos?

- ◯ ______
- ◯ ______
- ◯ ______

Other to-dos

Daily Schedule

Notes, issues, and reflections

DAILY NOTES

Date:

DAILY PLAN

Date:

☐ *Practice Stillness*

What are your 3 key to-dos?

○

○

○

Daily Schedule

Other to-dos

Notes, issues, and reflections

DAILY NOTES

Date:

DAILY PLAN

Date: ______

☐ *Practice Stillness*

What are your 3 key to-dos?

○ ______
○ ______
○ ______

Other to-dos

Daily Schedule

Notes, issues, and reflections

DAILY NOTES

Date:

The way to get started is to quit talking and begin doing.

—Walt Disney

CLARITY BREAK

Clarity Break Questions

- *Is the Vision and Plan for the business/department on track?*
- *What is the number one goal?*
- *Am I focusing on the most important things?*
- *Do I have the Right People in the Right Seats to grow?*
- *What is the one "people move" that I must make this quarter?*
- *How strong is my bench?*
- *If I lose a key player, do I have someone ready to fill the seat?*
- *Are my processes working well?*
- *What seems overly complicated that must be simplified?*
- *Do I understand what my direct reports truly love to do and are great at doing?*
- *Am I leveraging their strengths?*
- *What can I delegate to others in order to use my time more effectively?*
- *What can we do to be more proactive versus being reactive?*
- *What can I do to improve communication?*
- *What's my top priority this week? This month?*

CLARITY BREAK

CLARITY BREAK

WEEKLY REVIEW

Week of: ______________ to ______________

☐ *Review Level 10 Meeting notes* ☐ *Review Quarterly Rocks*

☐ *Review last week's calendar*

What worked last week:

What didn't work last week:

Knowing what you know now, what will you do differently next week?

What were your 3 biggest wins last week, and why?

Looking over the past week, what are you most grateful for?

WEEKLY PLAN

Week of: ____________ to ____________

☐ *Review V/TO* ☐ *Review Personal V/TO* ☐ *Review last week's notes and to-dos*

☐ *Clear all inboxes*

What are your 3 biggest wins for next week?

○ ______________________________

○ ______________________________

○ ______________________________

How many hours will you work next week?

How do you plan to eat next week?

How do you plan to exercise next week?

How do you plan to connect with friends and family next week?

What are your key appointments and ideal outcomes for next week?

Date and Time	Appointment	Desired outcome

DAILY PLAN

Date:

☐ *Practice Stillness*

What are your 3 key to-dos?

○

○

○

Other to-dos

Daily Schedule

Notes, issues, and reflections

DAILY NOTES

Date:

DAILY PLAN

Date:

☐ *Practice Stillness*

What are your 3 key to-dos?

○

○

○

Daily Schedule

Other to-dos

Notes, issues, and reflections

DAILY NOTES

Date: ______

DAILY PLAN

Date: ______

☐ *Practice Stillness*

What are your 3 key to-dos?

○ ______
○ ______
○ ______

Other to-dos

Daily Schedule

Notes, issues, and reflections

DAILY NOTES

Date: ____________

DAILY PLAN

Date:

☐ *Practice Stillness*

What are your 3 key to-dos?

○

○

○

Other to-dos

Daily Schedule

Notes, issues, and reflections

DAILY NOTES

Date:

DAILY PLAN

Date:

☐ *Practice Stillness*

What are your 3 key to-dos?

○

○

○

Other to-dos

Daily Schedule

Notes, issues, and reflections

DAILY NOTES

Date: ____________

DAILY PLAN

Date:

☐ *Practice Stillness*

What are your 3 key to-dos?

○

○

○

Other to-dos

Daily Schedule

Notes, issues, and reflections

DAILY NOTES

Date:

DAILY PLAN

Date: ______

☐ *Practice Stillness*

What are your 3 key to-dos?

○ ______
○ ______
○ ______

Other to-dos

Daily Schedule

Notes, issues, and reflections

DAILY NOTES

Date:

If you really want something,
you'll find a way. If you don't,
you'll find an excuse.

—Jim Rohn

CLARITY BREAK

Clarity Break Questions

- *Is the Vision and Plan for the business/department on track?*
- *What is the number one goal?*
- *Am I focusing on the most important things?*
- *Do I have the Right People in the Right Seats to grow?*
- *What is the one "people move" that I must make this quarter?*
- *How strong is my bench?*
- *If I lose a key player, do I have someone ready to fill the seat?*
- *Are my processes working well?*
- *What seems overly complicated that must be simplified?*
- *Do I understand what my direct reports truly love to do and are great at doing?*
- *Am I leveraging their strengths?*
- *What can I delegate to others in order to use my time more effectively?*
- *What can we do to be more proactive versus being reactive?*
- *What can I do to improve communication?*
- *What's my top priority this week? This month?*

CLARITY BREAK

CLARITY BREAK

WEEKLY REVIEW

Week of: ______ to ______

☐ *Review Level 10 Meeting notes*

☐ *Review Quarterly Rocks*

☐ *Review last week's calendar*

What worked last week:

What didn't work last week:

Knowing what you know now, what will you do differently next week?

What were your 3 biggest wins last week, and why?

Looking over the past week, what are you most grateful for?

WEEKLY PLAN

Week of: ______ to ______

☐ *Review V/TO* ☐ *Review Personal V/TO* ☐ *Review last week's notes and to-dos*
☐ *Clear all inboxes*

What are your 3 biggest wins for next week?

○ ______
○ ______
○ ______

How many hours will you work next week?

How do you plan to eat next week?

How do you plan to exercise next week?

How do you plan to connect with friends and family next week?

What are your key appointments and ideal outcomes for next week?

Date and Time	Appointment	Desired outcome

DAILY PLAN

Date:

☐ *Practice Stillness*

What are your 3 key to-dos?

○
○
○

Other to-dos

Daily Schedule

Notes, issues, and reflections

DAILY NOTES

Date:

DAILY PLAN

Date:

☐ *Practice Stillness*

What are your 3 key to-dos?

○
○
○

Other to-dos

Daily Schedule

Notes, issues, and reflections

DAILY NOTES

Date:

DAILY PLAN

Date: ______

☐ *Practice Stillness*

What are your 3 key to-dos?

○ ______
○ ______
○ ______

Other to-dos

Daily Schedule

Notes, issues, and reflections

DAILY NOTES

Date:

DAILY PLAN

Date: ____________

☐ *Practice Stillness*

What are your 3 key to-dos?

○ ____________

○ ____________

○ ____________

Other to-dos

Daily Schedule

Notes, issues, and reflections

DAILY NOTES

Date:

DAILY PLAN

Date:

☐ *Practice Stillness*

What are your 3 key to-dos?

◯

◯

◯

Other to-dos

Daily Schedule

Notes, issues, and reflections

DAILY NOTES

Date: ____________

DAILY PLAN

Date: ____________

☐ *Practice Stillness*

What are your 3 key to-dos?

○ ____________
○ ____________
○ ____________

Other to-dos

Daily Schedule

Notes, issues, and reflections

DAILY NOTES

Date:

DAILY PLAN

Date: ____________

☐ *Practice Stillness*

What are your 3 key to-dos?

◯

◯

◯

Daily Schedule

Other to-dos

Notes, issues, and reflections

DAILY NOTES

Date:

Fall seven times and
stand up eight.

—Japanese proverb

CLARITY BREAK

Clarity Break Questions

- *Is the Vision and Plan for the business/department on track?*
- *What is the number one goal?*
- *Am I focusing on the most important things?*
- *Do I have the Right People in the Right Seats to grow?*
- *What is the one "people move" that I must make this quarter?*
- *How strong is my bench?*
- *If I lose a key player, do I have someone ready to fill the seat?*
- *Are my processes working well?*
- *What seems overly complicated that must be simplified?*
- *Do I understand what my direct reports truly love to do and are great at doing?*
- *Am I leveraging their strengths?*
- *What can I delegate to others in order to use my time more effectively?*
- *What can we do to be more proactive versus being reactive?*
- *What can I do to improve communication?*
- *What's my top priority this week? This month?*

CLARITY BREAK

CLARITY BREAK

WEEKLY REVIEW

Week of: ________ to ________

☐ *Review Level 10 Meeting notes*

☐ *Review Quarterly Rocks*

☐ *Review last week's calendar*

What worked last week:

What didn't work last week:

Knowing what you know now, what will you do differently next week?

What were your 3 biggest wins last week, and why?

Looking over the past week, what are you most grateful for?

WEEKLY PLAN

Week of: ____________ to ____________

☐ *Review V/TO* ☐ *Review Personal V/TO* ☐ *Review last week's notes and to-dos*

☐ *Clear all inboxes*

What are your 3 biggest wins for next week?

○ ____________

○ ____________

○ ____________

How many hours will you work next week?

How do you plan to eat next week?

How do you plan to exercise next week?

How do you plan to connect with friends and family next week?

What are your key appointments and ideal outcomes for next week?

Date and Time	Appointment	Desired outcome

DAILY PLAN

Date: __________

☐ *Practice Stillness*

What are your 3 key to-dos?

○ __________

○ __________

○ __________

Other to-dos

Daily Schedule

Notes, issues, and reflections

DAILY NOTES

Date: ______

DAILY PLAN

Date:

☐ *Practice Stillness*

What are your 3 key to-dos?

○

○

○

Daily Schedule

Other to-dos

Notes, issues, and reflections

DAILY NOTES

Date: ______________

DAILY PLAN

Date: ______________

☐ *Practice Stillness*

What are your 3 key to-dos?

○ ______________

○ ______________

○ ______________

Other to-dos

Daily Schedule

Notes, issues, and reflections

DAILY NOTES

Date:

DAILY PLAN

Date:

☐ *Practice Stillness*

What are your 3 key to-dos?

○

○

○

Other to-dos

Daily Schedule

Notes, issues, and reflections

DAILY NOTES

Date:

DAILY PLAN

Date: ____________

☐ *Practice Stillness*

What are your 3 key to-dos?

◯ ____________

◯ ____________

◯ ____________

Other to-dos

Daily Schedule

Notes, issues, and reflections

DAILY NOTES

Date: ____________

DAILY PLAN

Date:

☐ *Practice Stillness*

What are your 3 key to-dos?

○

○

○

Other to-dos

Daily Schedule

Notes, issues, and reflections

DAILY NOTES

Date:

DAILY PLAN

Date:

☐ *Practice Stillness*

What are your 3 key to-dos?

○

○

○

Other to-dos

Daily Schedule

Notes, issues, and reflections

DAILY NOTES

Date:

In every day, there are 1,440 minutes. That means we have 1,440 daily opportunities to make a positive impact.

—Les Brown

CLARITY BREAK

Clarity Break Questions

- *Is the Vision and Plan for the business/department on track?*
- *What is the number one goal?*
- *Am I focusing on the most important things?*
- *Do I have the Right People in the Right Seats to grow?*
- *What is the one "people move" that I must make this quarter?*
- *How strong is my bench?*
- *If I lose a key player, do I have someone ready to fill the seat?*
- *Are my processes working well?*
- *What seems overly complicated that must be simplified?*
- *Do I understand what my direct reports truly love to do and are great at doing?*
- *Am I leveraging their strengths?*
- *What can I delegate to others in order to use my time more effectively?*
- *What can we do to be more proactive versus being reactive?*
- *What can I do to improve communication?*
- *What's my top priority this week? This month?*

CLARITY BREAK

CLARITY BREAK

WEEKLY REVIEW

Week of: ______ to ______

☐ *Review Level 10 Meeting notes*

☐ *Review Quarterly Rocks*

☐ *Review last week's calendar*

What worked last week:

What didn't work last week:

Knowing what you know now, what will you do differently next week?

What were your 3 biggest wins last week, and why?

Looking over the past week, what are you most grateful for?

WEEKLY PLAN

Week of: ______ to ______

☐ *Review V/TO* ☐ *Review Personal V/TO* ☐ *Review last week's notes and to-dos*

☐ *Clear all inboxes*

What are your 3 biggest wins for next week?

○ ______

○ ______

○ ______

How many hours will you work next week?

How do you plan to eat next week?

How do you plan to exercise next week?

How do you plan to connect with friends and family next week?

What are your key appointments and ideal outcomes for next week?

Date and Time	Appointment	Desired outcome

DAILY PLAN

Date: ____________

☐ *Practice Stillness*

What are your 3 key to-dos?

○ ____________

○ ____________

○ ____________

Other to-dos

Daily Schedule

Notes, issues, and reflections

DAILY NOTES

Date: ______________

DAILY PLAN

Date: ______________

☐ *Practice Stillness*

What are your 3 key to-dos?

◯ ______________

◯ ______________

◯ ______________

Other to-dos

Daily Schedule

Notes, issues, and reflections

DAILY NOTES

Date: ____________

DAILY PLAN

Date:

☐ *Practice Stillness*

What are your 3 key to-dos?

○

○

○

Other to-dos

Daily Schedule

Notes, issues, and reflections

DAILY NOTES

Date:

DAILY PLAN

Date:

☐ *Practice Stillness*

What are your 3 key to-dos?

○

○

○

Other to-dos

Daily Schedule

Notes, issues, and reflections

DAILY NOTES

Date: ____________

DAILY PLAN

Date: ____________

☐ *Practice Stillness*

What are your 3 key to-dos?

○ ____________

○ ____________

○ ____________

Other to-dos

Daily Schedule

Notes, issues, and reflections

DAILY NOTES

Date:

DAILY PLAN

Date: ______

☐ *Practice Stillness*

What are your 3 key to-dos?

○

○

○

Other to-dos

Daily Schedule

Notes, issues, and reflections

DAILY NOTES

Date: ______________

DAILY PLAN

Date: ____________

☐ *Practice Stillness*

What are your 3 key to-dos?

○ ____________

○ ____________

○ ____________

Other to-dos

Daily Schedule

Notes, issues, and reflections

DAILY NOTES

Date: __________

There is no easy walk to freedom anywhere, and many of us will have to pass through the valley of the shadow of death again and again before we reach the mountaintop of our desires.

—Nelson Mandela

CLARITY BREAK

Clarity Break Questions

- *Is the Vision and Plan for the business/department on track?*
- *What is the number one goal?*
- *Am I focusing on the most important things?*
- *Do I have the Right People in the Right Seats to grow?*
- *What is the one "people move" that I must make this quarter?*
- *How strong is my bench?*
- *If I lose a key player, do I have someone ready to fill the seat?*
- *Are my processes working well?*
- *What seems overly complicated that must be simplified?*
- *Do I understand what my direct reports truly love to do and are great at doing?*
- *Am I leveraging their strengths?*
- *What can I delegate to others in order to use my time more effectively?*
- *What can we do to be more proactive versus being reactive?*
- *What can I do to improve communication?*
- *What's my top priority this week? This month?*

CLARITY BREAK

CLARITY BREAK

WEEKLY REVIEW

Week of: __________ to __________

☐ *Review Level 10 Meeting notes* ☐ *Review Quarterly Rocks*

☐ *Review last week's calendar*

What worked last week:

What didn't work last week:

Knowing what you know now, what will you do differently next week?

What were your 3 biggest wins last week, and why?

Looking over the past week, what are you most grateful for?

WEEKLY PLAN

Week of: ______ to ______

☐ *Review V/TO* ☐ *Review Personal V/TO* ☐ *Review last week's notes and to-dos*
☐ *Clear all inboxes*

What are your 3 biggest wins for next week?

○ ______
○ ______
○ ______

How many hours will you work next week?

How do you plan to eat next week?

How do you plan to exercise next week?

How do you plan to connect with friends and family next week?

What are your key appointments and ideal outcomes for next week?

Date and Time	Appointment	Desired outcome

DAILY PLAN

Date:

☐ *Practice Stillness*

What are your 3 key to-dos?

○

○

○

Other to-dos

Daily Schedule

Notes, issues, and reflections

DAILY NOTES

Date:

DAILY PLAN

Date: ______

☐ *Practice Stillness*

What are your 3 key to-dos?

○ ______
○ ______
○ ______

Other to-dos

Daily Schedule

Notes, issues, and reflections

DAILY NOTES

Date:

DAILY PLAN

Date: ______

☐ *Practice Stillness*

What are your 3 key to-dos?

○ ______

○ ______

○ ______

Other to-dos

Daily Schedule

Notes, issues, and reflections

DAILY NOTES

Date:

DAILY PLAN

Date:

☐ *Practice Stillness*

What are your 3 key to-dos?

○
○
○

Daily Schedule

Other to-dos

Notes, issues, and reflections

DAILY NOTES

Date: ____________

DAILY PLAN

Date:

☐ *Practice Stillness*

What are your 3 key to-dos?

○

○

○

Daily Schedule

Other to-dos

Notes, issues, and reflections

DAILY NOTES

Date: ______

DAILY PLAN

Date: ______

☐ *Practice Stillness*

What are your 3 key to-dos?

○ ______
○ ______
○ ______

Other to-dos

Daily Schedule

Notes, issues, and reflections

DAILY NOTES

Date:

DAILY PLAN

Date:

☐ *Practice Stillness*

What are your 3 key to-dos?

◯

◯

◯

Daily Schedule

Other to-dos

Notes, issues, and reflections

DAILY NOTES

Date:

Be thankful for what you have; you'll end up having more. If you concentrate on what you don't have, you will never, ever have enough.

—Oprah Winfrey

CLARITY BREAK

Clarity Break Questions

- *Is the Vision and Plan for the business/department on track?*
- *What is the number one goal?*
- *Am I focusing on the most important things?*
- *Do I have the Right People in the Right Seats to grow?*
- *What is the one "people move" that I must make this quarter?*
- *How strong is my bench?*
- *If I lose a key player, do I have someone ready to fill the seat?*
- *Are my processes working well?*
- *What seems overly complicated that must be simplified?*
- *Do I understand what my direct reports truly love to do and are great at doing?*
- *Am I leveraging their strengths?*
- *What can I delegate to others in order to use my time more effectively?*
- *What can we do to be more proactive versus being reactive?*
- *What can I do to improve communication?*
- *What's my top priority this week? This month?*

CLARITY BREAK

CLARITY BREAK

WEEKLY REVIEW

Week of: ________ to ________

☐ *Review Level 10 Meeting notes*

☐ *Review Quarterly Rocks*

☐ *Review last week's calendar*

What worked last week:

What didn't work last week:

Knowing what you know now, what will you do differently next week?

What were your 3 biggest wins last week, and why?

Looking over the past week, what are you most grateful for?

WEEKLY PLAN

Week of: ______ to ______

☐ *Review V/TO* ☐ *Review Personal V/TO* ☐ *Review last week's notes and to-dos*

☐ *Clear all inboxes*

What are your 3 biggest wins for next week?

◯ ______

◯ ______

◯ ______

How many hours will you work next week?

How do you plan to eat next week?

How do you plan to exercise next week?

How do you plan to connect with friends and family next week?

What are your key appointments and ideal outcomes for next week?

Date and Time	Appointment	Desired outcome

DAILY PLAN

Date: ____________

☐ *Practice Stillness*

What are your 3 key to-dos?

○ ____________
○ ____________
○ ____________

Other to-dos

Daily Schedule

Notes, issues, and reflections

DAILY NOTES

Date: ____________

DAILY PLAN

Date: ____________

☐ *Practice Stillness*

What are your 3 key to-dos?

◯ ____________

◯ ____________

◯ ____________

Other to-dos

Daily Schedule

Notes, issues, and reflections

DAILY NOTES

Date:

DAILY PLAN

Date:

☐ *Practice Stillness*

What are your 3 key to-dos?

○

○

○

Other to-dos

Daily Schedule

Notes, issues, and reflections

DAILY NOTES

Date:

DAILY PLAN

Date: __________

☐ *Practice Stillness*

What are your 3 key to-dos?

○ __________

○ __________

○ __________

Other to-dos

Daily Schedule

Notes, issues, and reflections

DAILY NOTES

Date:

DAILY PLAN

Date: ____________

☐ *Practice Stillness*

What are your 3 key to-dos?

○ ____________

○ ____________

○ ____________

Other to-dos

Daily Schedule

Notes, issues, and reflections

DAILY NOTES

Date:

DAILY PLAN

Date:

☐ *Practice Stillness*

What are your 3 key to-dos?

○

○

○

Other to-dos

Daily Schedule

Notes, issues, and reflections

DAILY NOTES

Date:

DAILY PLAN

Date:

☐ *Practice Stillness*

What are your 3 key to-dos?

◯

◯

◯

Other to-dos

Daily Schedule

Notes, issues, and reflections

DAILY NOTES

Date:

The truth is that all of us are already 100% self-disciplined—to our existing set of habits.

—Dan Sullivan

CLARITY BREAK

Clarity Break Questions

- *Is the Vision and Plan for the business/ department on track?*
- *What is the number one goal?*
- *Am I focusing on the most important things?*
- *Do I have the Right People in the Right Seats to grow?*
- *What is the one "people move" that I must make this quarter?*
- *How strong is my bench?*
- *If I lose a key player, do I have someone ready to fill the seat?*
- *Are my processes working well?*
- *What seems overly complicated that must be simplified?*
- *Do I understand what my direct reports truly love to do and are great at doing?*
- *Am I leveraging their strengths?*
- *What can I delegate to others in order to use my time more effectively?*
- *What can we do to be more proactive versus being reactive?*
- *What can I do to improve communication?*
- *What's my top priority this week? This month?*

CLARITY BREAK

CLARITY BREAK

WEEKLY REVIEW

Week of: ______ to ______

☐ *Review Level 10 Meeting notes*

☐ *Review Quarterly Rocks*

☐ *Review last week's calendar*

What worked last week:

What didn't work last week:

Knowing what you know now, what will you do differently next week?

What were your 3 biggest wins last week, and why?

Looking over the past week, what are you most grateful for?

WEEKLY PLAN

Week of: ____________ to ____________

☐ *Review V/TO* ☐ *Review Personal V/TO* ☐ *Review last week's notes and to-dos*

☐ *Clear all inboxes*

What are your 3 biggest wins for next week?

◯ ____________

◯ ____________

◯ ____________

How many hours will you work next week?

How do you plan to eat next week?

How do you plan to exercise next week?

How do you plan to connect with friends and family next week?

What are your key appointments and ideal outcomes for next week?

Date and Time	Appointment	Desired outcome

DAILY PLAN

Date: ____________

☐ *Practice Stillness*

What are your 3 key to-dos?

○ ____________

○ ____________

○ ____________

Other to-dos

Daily Schedule

Notes, issues, and reflections

DAILY NOTES

Date:

DAILY PLAN

Date:

☐ *Practice Stillness*

What are your 3 key to-dos?

◯

◯

◯

Daily Schedule

Other to-dos

Notes, issues, and reflections

DAILY NOTES

Date:

DAILY PLAN

Date:

☐ *Practice Stillness*

What are your 3 key to-dos?

○

○

○

Other to-dos

Daily Schedule

Notes, issues, and reflections

DAILY NOTES

Date:

DAILY PLAN

Date: ____________

☐ *Practice Stillness*

What are your 3 key to-dos?

○ ____________

○ ____________

○ ____________

Other to-dos

Daily Schedule

Notes, issues, and reflections

DAILY NOTES

Date:

DAILY PLAN

Date:

☐ *Practice Stillness*

What are your 3 key to-dos?

○

○

○

Other to-dos

Daily Schedule

Notes, issues, and reflections

DAILY NOTES

Date: ______

DAILY PLAN

Date: ____________

☐ *Practice Stillness*

What are your 3 key to-dos?

○ ____________

○ ____________

○ ____________

Other to-dos

Daily Schedule

Notes, issues, and reflections

DAILY NOTES

Date:

DAILY PLAN

Date: ____________

☐ *Practice Stillness*

What are your 3 key to-dos?

○ ____________

○ ____________

○ ____________

Other to-dos

Daily Schedule

Notes, issues, and reflections

DAILY NOTES

Date: ______

Whether you think you can or think you can't, you're right.

—Henry Ford

CLARITY BREAK

Clarity Break Questions

- *Is the Vision and Plan for the business/department on track?*
- *What is the number one goal?*
- *Am I focusing on the most important things?*
- *Do I have the Right People in the Right Seats to grow?*
- *What is the one "people move" that I must make this quarter?*
- *How strong is my bench?*
- *If I lose a key player, do I have someone ready to fill the seat?*
- *Are my processes working well?*
- *What seems overly complicated that must be simplified?*
- *Do I understand what my direct reports truly love to do and are great at doing?*
- *Am I leveraging their strengths?*
- *What can I delegate to others in order to use my time more effectively?*
- *What can we do to be more proactive versus being reactive?*
- *What can I do to improve communication?*
- *What's my top priority this week? This month?*

CLARITY BREAK

CLARITY BREAK

WEEKLY REVIEW

Week of: ________ to ________

☐ *Review Level 10 Meeting notes* ☐ *Review Quarterly Rocks*

☐ *Review last week's calendar*

What worked last week:

What didn't work last week:

Knowing what you know now, what will you do differently next week?

What were your 3 biggest wins last week, and why?

Looking over the past week, what are you most grateful for?

WEEKLY PLAN

Week of: ______ to ______

☐ *Review V/TO* ☐ *Review Personal V/TO* ☐ *Review last week's notes and to-dos*
☐ *Clear all inboxes*

What are your 3 biggest wins for next week?

○ ______
○ ______
○ ______

How many hours will you work next week?

How do you plan to eat next week?

How do you plan to exercise next week?

How do you plan to connect with friends and family next week?

What are your key appointments and ideal outcomes for next week?

Date and Time	Appointment	Desired outcome

DAILY PLAN

Date: ____________

☐ *Practice Stillness*

What are your 3 key to-dos?

○ ____________

○ ____________

○ ____________

Other to-dos

Daily Schedule

Notes, issues, and reflections

DAILY NOTES

Date:

DAILY PLAN

Date:

☐ *Practice Stillness*

What are your 3 key to-dos?

○
○
○

Other to-dos

Daily Schedule

Notes, issues, and reflections

DAILY NOTES

Date:

DAILY PLAN

Date:

☐ *Practice Stillness*

What are your 3 key to-dos?

- ◯
- ◯
- ◯

Other to-dos

Daily Schedule

Notes, issues, and reflections

DAILY NOTES

Date:

DAILY PLAN

Date:

☐ *Practice Stillness*

What are your 3 key to-dos?

○
○
○

Daily Schedule

Other to-dos

Notes, issues, and reflections

DAILY NOTES

Date:

DAILY PLAN

Date: ______

☐ *Practice Stillness*

What are your 3 key to-dos?

○ ______
○ ______
○ ______

Other to-dos

Daily Schedule

Notes, issues, and reflections

DAILY NOTES

Date:

DAILY PLAN

Date:

☐ *Practice Stillness*

What are your 3 key to-dos?

○

○

○

Other to-dos

Daily Schedule

Notes, issues, and reflections

DAILY NOTES

Date:

DAILY PLAN

Date:

☐ *Practice Stillness*

What are your 3 key to-dos?

○

○

○

Daily Schedule

Other to-dos

Notes, issues, and reflections

DAILY NOTES

Date:

Security is mostly a superstition.
Life is either a daring
adventure or nothing.

—Helen Keller

CLARITY BREAK

Clarity Break Questions

- *Is the Vision and Plan for the business/department on track?*
- *What is the number one goal?*
- *Am I focusing on the most important things?*
- *Do I have the Right People in the Right Seats to grow?*
- *What is the one "people move" that I must make this quarter?*
- *How strong is my bench?*
- *If I lose a key player, do I have someone ready to fill the seat?*
- *Are my processes working well?*
- *What seems overly complicated that must be simplified?*
- *Do I understand what my direct reports truly love to do and are great at doing?*
- *Am I leveraging their strengths?*
- *What can I delegate to others in order to use my time more effectively?*
- *What can we do to be more proactive versus being reactive?*
- *What can I do to improve communication?*
- *What's my top priority this week? This month?*

CLARITY BREAK

CLARITY BREAK

WEEKLY REVIEW

Week of: ______________ to ______________

☐ *Review Level 10 Meeting notes*

☐ *Review Quarterly Rocks*

☐ *Review last week's calendar*

What worked last week:

What didn't work last week:

Knowing what you know now, what will you do differently next week?

What were your 3 biggest wins last week, and why?

Looking over the past week, what are you most grateful for?

WEEKLY PLAN

Week of: ____________ to ____________

☐ *Review V/TO* ☐ *Review Personal V/TO* ☐ *Review last week's notes and to-dos*
☐ *Clear all inboxes*

What are your 3 biggest wins for next week?

◯ ____________
◯ ____________
◯ ____________

How many hours will you work next week?

How do you plan to eat next week?

How do you plan to exercise next week?

How do you plan to connect with friends and family next week?

What are your key appointments and ideal outcomes for next week?

Date and Time	Appointment	Desired outcome

DAILY PLAN

Date:

☐ *Practice Stillness*

What are your 3 key to-dos?

○

○

○

Other to-dos

Daily Schedule

Notes, issues, and reflections

DAILY NOTES

Date: ______________

DAILY PLAN

Date: ____________

☐ *Practice Stillness*

What are your 3 key to-dos?

○ ____________

○ ____________

○ ____________

Other to-dos

Daily Schedule

Notes, issues, and reflections

DAILY NOTES

Date: ______________________

DAILY PLAN

Date: ____________

☐ *Practice Stillness*

What are your 3 key to-dos?

○ ____________
○ ____________
○ ____________

Other to-dos

Daily Schedule

Notes, issues, and reflections

DAILY NOTES

Date:

DAILY PLAN

Date:

☐ *Practice Stillness*

What are your 3 key to-dos?

○
○
○

Other to-dos

Daily Schedule

Notes, issues, and reflections

DAILY NOTES

Date: ____________

DAILY PLAN

Date:

☐ *Practice Stillness*

What are your 3 key to-dos?

- ◯
- ◯
- ◯

Other to-dos

Daily Schedule

Notes, issues, and reflections

DAILY NOTES

Date:

DAILY PLAN

Date:

☐ *Practice Stillness*

What are your 3 key to-dos?

○

○

○

Other to-dos

Daily Schedule

Notes, issues, and reflections

DAILY NOTES

Date:

DAILY PLAN

Date:

☐ *Practice Stillness*

What are your 3 key to-dos?

○

○

○

Other to-dos

Daily Schedule

Notes, issues, and reflections

DAILY NOTES

Date:

The man who has confidence in himself gains the confidence of others.

—Hasidic proverb

CLARITY BREAK

Clarity Break Questions

- *Is the Vision and Plan for the business/department on track?*
- *What is the number one goal?*
- *Am I focusing on the most important things?*
- *Do I have the Right People in the Right Seats to grow?*
- *What is the one "people move" that I must make this quarter?*
- *How strong is my bench?*
- *If I lose a key player, do I have someone ready to fill the seat?*
- *Are my processes working well?*
- *What seems overly complicated that must be simplified?*
- *Do I understand what my direct reports truly love to do and are great at doing?*
- *Am I leveraging their strengths?*
- *What can I delegate to others in order to use my time more effectively?*
- *What can we do to be more proactive versus being reactive?*
- *What can I do to improve communication?*
- *What's my top priority this week? This month?*

CLARITY BREAK

CLARITY BREAK

WEEKLY REVIEW

Week of: ______________ to ______________

☐ *Review Level 10 Meeting notes*

☐ *Review Quarterly Rocks*

☐ *Review last week's calendar*

What worked last week:

What didn't work last week:

Knowing what you know now, what will you do differently next week?

What were your 3 biggest wins last week, and why?

Looking over the past week, what are you most grateful for?

WEEKLY PLAN

Week of: ______ to ______

☐ *Review V/TO* ☐ *Review Personal V/TO* ☐ *Review last week's notes and to-dos*
☐ *Clear all inboxes*

What are your 3 biggest wins for next week?

○ ______
○ ______
○ ______

How many hours will you work next week?

How do you plan to eat next week?

How do you plan to exercise next week?

How do you plan to connect with friends and family next week?

What are your key appointments and ideal outcomes for next week?

Date and Time	Appointment	Desired outcome

DAILY PLAN

Date: ____________

☐ *Practice Stillness*

What are your 3 key to-dos?

○ ____________

○ ____________

○ ____________

Other to-dos

Daily Schedule

Notes, issues, and reflections

DAILY NOTES

Date: __________

DAILY PLAN

Date: ______

☐ *Practice Stillness*

What are your 3 key to-dos?

○ ______
○ ______
○ ______

Other to-dos

Daily Schedule

Notes, issues, and reflections

DAILY NOTES

Date:

DAILY PLAN

Date: ______________

☐ *Practice Stillness*

What are your 3 key to-dos?

◯ ______________
◯ ______________
◯ ______________

Other to-dos

Daily Schedule

Notes, issues, and reflections

DAILY NOTES

Date:

DAILY PLAN

Date: ______

☐ *Practice Stillness*

What are your 3 key to-dos?

◯ ______
◯ ______
◯ ______

Other to-dos

Daily Schedule

Notes, issues, and reflections

DAILY NOTES

Date: ____________

DAILY PLAN

Date: ______

☐ *Practice Stillness*

What are your 3 key to-dos?

◯ ______

◯ ______

◯ ______

Other to-dos

Daily Schedule

Notes, issues, and reflections

DAILY NOTES

Date:

DAILY PLAN

Date:

☐ *Practice Stillness*

What are your 3 key to-dos?

○

○

○

Other to-dos

Daily Schedule

Notes, issues, and reflections

DAILY NOTES

Date: ______________

DAILY PLAN

Date:

☐ *Practice Stillness*

What are your 3 key to-dos?

○

○

○

Other to-dos

Daily Schedule

Notes, issues, and reflections

DAILY NOTES

Date: ______________

Don't let yesterday take up too much of today.

—Will Rogers

QUARTERLY CONVERSATION NOTES

QUARTERLY CONVERSATION NOTES

QUARTERLY CONVERSATION NOTES

QUARTERLY CONVERSATION NOTES

QUARTERLY CONVERSATION NOTES

QUARTERLY CONVERSATION NOTES

QUARTERLY CONVERSATION NOTES

QUARTERLY CONVERSATION NOTES

QUARTERLY CONVERSATION NOTES

QUARTERLY CONVERSATION NOTES

QUARTERLY CONVERSATION NOTES

QUARTERLY CONVERSATION NOTES

QUARTERLY CONVERSATION NOTES

QUARTERLY CONVERSATION NOTES

QUARTERLY PLANNING NOTES

QUARTERLY PLANNING NOTES

GENERAL NOTES

GENERAL NOTES